SHERWOOD ANDERSON

From a Painting by Karl Anderson

SHERWOOD ANDERSON

By
CLEVELAND B. CHASE

HASKELL HOUSE PUBLISHERS LTD.
Publishers of Scarce Scholarly Books
NEW YORK, N. Y. 10012
1972

HASKELL HOUSE PUBLISHERS Ltd.

Publishers of Scarce Scholarly Books

280 LAFAYETTE STREET

NEW YORK, N. Y. 10012

Library of Congress Cataloging in Publication Data

Chase, Cleveland Bruce, 1903-
    Sherwood Anderson.

    Original ed. issued in series: Modern American
writers.
    Bibliography: p.
    1. Anderson, Sherwood, 1876-1941.
PS3501.N4Z56 1972   813'.5'2   72-3565
ISBN 0-8383-1543-7

Printed in the United States of America

TO

FRANK E. HILL

CONTENTS

SHERWOOD ANDERSON

Sherwood Anderson

I. ABOUT AMERICA AND ANDERSON

NOTHING could be more indicative of the intimate relation between literature and sociological conditions than the literary renascence we have gone through in the past decade or two. Had that renascence been dependent upon the perceptive genius of a single great writer, such a generalization might be suspect. But to the contrary it has been the work of a dozen or more writers all conscious of practically the same limitations in their artistic environment, all feeling the need of expressing new sentiments and of a fresh medium for expression, all of them excited by the possibilities of creating a new art, a dozen writers groping blindly, impatiently, often with pathetic inadequacy to discover and interpret their feelings about life.

To venture into the dangerous and unproductive field of prediction, I would guess that not one of these authors will be read fifty years hence. Few, if any of them, are of extraordinary talent. But most of them are honest, they are persistent, and in their attempt to bring writing back into

1

contact with reality and to divorce it from com-
merce and the exigencies of eonomic necessity they
are building a foundation for the first real and
valid American literature.

Before these writers appeared it was mere
quibbling to attempt to differentiate between
English and American literature. What differences there were between the two were far more
in degree than in kind. The only American writing not directly inspired by England was the
wholesale production of optimism and moralizing
manufactured to suit the dual necessities of a
Puritan race that had set for itself the goal of
subduing a rich and barren country.

While we were still making ourselves the big-
gest and richest machine in the world, pessimism
could be and had to be stifled. Writing, like religion, was made a subordinate servant to com-
merce and pioneering progress. Its allotted tasks
were to disseminate optimism and to preach the
ideal of progress. To toil-worn pioneers whose
lives were built upon hopes for the future, cheerful optimistic delusions were a necessity. Progress, to them, was the most concrete of facts—so
many acres of land cleared and put under culti-
vation, so many miles of railroad built, so many
more factories producing, so many more dollars'
worth of goods. Everything that men thought
about and worked for could be measured in material scales. Abstractions did not enter people's
lives. Even religion had been made concrete.
People were either good or bad—good if they con-

formed to certain rules of morality, bad if they broke them. And this moral code was soon made to coincide with the necessities of a pioneering country.

And America remained in spirit a pioneer country, preoccupied with the mechanics of life, until quite recently. It was not until we had succeeded in cornering a large part of the material wealth and power of the world that most of us realized that the days of extravagant expansion were over. Instead of boasting of "God's country" we began to travel patronizingly through Europe; we hushed up "the land of the free," and the "melting pot" ideas and passed prohibition and immigration laws; extravagant speech about what we were going to do gave way to "back to normalcy"; Roosevelt was replaced by Coolidge. The economic conquest over, writers began to use their imaginations in an attempt to understand and interpret what they actually saw around them, rather than in the less difficult task of creating a fictitious world of illusion.

This change took place during the first quarter of the present century. We might conveniently date its beginning with the publication in 1900 of Dreiser's *Sister Carrie* and its culmination with the recent 100,000 sale of the same author's *The American Tragedy*. What more natural than that writers no longer forced by public opinion to be cheerful, should give way to a burst of disillusion, pessimism and criticism, and should search out and note down cold and often unpleasant facts

about life and people? It is unthinkable that at
such a time we should not find our Menckens and
Sinclair Lewises to snap and snarl at and worry
the creature of skin and bones that was once the
irresistible pachyderm of our pioneer ancestors.

Of the three important writers of fiction this
period has produced, Sherwood Anderson is the
only non-journalist. Sinclair Lewis has set down
in a sadly incomplete Doomsday Book some of the
phenomena to be found within our borders; he has
monotonously   described   the   movements   and
actions of some of our compatriots; he has said
nothing pertinent or valid about the people themselves. Dreiser has labored and out of the mountain of his humorless journalism has come forth
a mouse, but the mouse is alive and worth attention for that reason, if for no other.

Sherwood Anderson is something of an anom-
aly. He has been more daring than any of
his contemporaries in his attempts to get to the
basic facts about people. He has tried to explore
deeper into human emotions and reactions than
they. He has tried to seize upon the important,
significant moments in the dull and drab lives that
go on about him. In his search for the until recently disguised facts about modern life, and in
his statement of human problems he stands shoulder to shoulder with the best of his contemporaries
the world over. But if he has attempted much, he
has often failed. In his disposal of these facts and
in his interpretation of these problems he often
goes as far off the track as did the writers of the

old Pollyanna school. His work contains more sentimental alloy than that of any other "serious" modern writer. More than any of them he has fallen back upon the trick of his Puritan ancestors of denying the present and escaping into a fictitious world that never was and never will be. True, his world is not that of the Puritans, but at times it seems as far from reality as theirs.

It is an interesting and rather sad study to see Anderson skirt the edges of great writing only to slip back with a regularity that becomes monotonous into the second-rate. Often one gets the impression that he "feels" great writing, but lacks the inner hardness and determination necessary to express it.

In writing about one of George Bellows' paintings he once said, "You get back to the people painted by Mr. Bellows and forget him and that is as it should be. That is what the artist intends and wants when he is really feeling the thing on which he is at work." That quality one never gets in Sherwood Anderson's writing. Often he conceives a character with perfect integrity and objectiveness, but before he has finished he must project his own incongruous personality into the picture—and often he loses sight of his first conception in a growing preoccupation with himself or with some of his personal problems.

Anderson is intelligent and sensitive enough to realize what is happening to people in America. As a result he conceives his characters validly. Both they and their problems are real. But he

can't go through with them. Having uncovered
the truth, he lacks the courage to face it. Ar-
rived at that point he either (if he is writing
about himself) asks how he can be expected to
persevere against such odds as face a writer in the
modern world, or else he floats away from the un-
pleasantness of life on the wings of sentimentality.

It is this quality in Anderson that accounts for
the striking way in which his works start strongly
and gradually peter out. The same thing happens in each of his novels and in most of his short
stories. To understand why this is so, one must
know something of the man.

If it is easy—perhaps too easy—to become an-
noyed with Anderson, the writer who gives so
much promise and so little else, it is difficult not
to feel sympathetic toward the man.

According to an authorized statement, "He
was born in the Ohio village of Camden in 1876,
the third of a family of five boys and two girls.
The boys are all living, the two girls dead. The
family was a drifting, gypsy kind of tribe, headed
by one Irwin Anderson, the son of some broken
Southern family. As to the family ancestry it is
uncertain. The father of the family, known as
Ted, the Major, the Captain, the Colonel, was a
great talker and story teller. Sometimes he told
stories of old Irish kings who were his ancestors,
sometimes of Italian Barons. To add a touch
of realism to the tales he constantly told he represented himself as coming from a slave-holding

family of South Carolina, as being a mountain man of North Carolina, as being whatever figure would most enhance his tale. Sherwood Anderson has built many tales about this man. He was a slender man with a black mustache and a hat worn jauntily on the side of his head. Fond of drinking, good food, gaudy clothes and company, he was seldom at home. In his wanderings this man had married a slender, dark, handsome girl about whom little is known. She died at an early age but left a deep impression on all of her sons."

Sherwood Anderson's own boyhood was spent in the village of Clyde, Ohio, where he performed the usual round of odd jobs that fall to the lot of an energetic and capable poor boy in a Middle-Western village. Occasionally he went to school, but more often he loitered in bar rooms, stores and livery stables picking up funds of information and observation that stuck in his sensitive mind. After his mother's death, when he was fourteen, the family broke up rapidly and Sherwood wandered about the Middle-West as a laborer, a race-track follower, tramp and factory hand.

The Spanish American war seems to have been a turning point of a sort in his life. He enlisted frankly for the excitement and change. "To my amazement," he writes, "when I returned to my home town to become a soldier I was greeted as a hero—one who had given up a lucrative position in the city in order to fight for his country. My natural shrewdness led me to take advantage of this situation and I enjoyed it thoroughly." He

followed up this advantage and, after his demo-
bilization, returned to Ohio, married and settled
down. He proved to be a thoroughly competent
business man, able to handle men and sell goods,
and not long afterward we find him the president
of a paint manufacturing concern in Elyria, Ohio.
He remained there until about 1910.

These years gave a final direction to Anderson's
life. Succumbing to the lure of business, he went
at it harder and expected more of it than a man
of less imagination would have. It offered a point
of orientation for his disordered life. He succeeded, succeeded perhaps too easily, for in his
success there was no grain of satisfaction. Due to
the vividness of his romantic imagination, the
struggle to reach the top had occupied his whole
being, but once there he discovered somewhat to
his surprise that the buying and selling of mate-
rials was a mechanical process and had little connection with his real interests. His imagination
demanded something else upon which to fix its
attention, and the lot fell to writing.

Anderson's experience in business was not
greatly different from that of many American
men during the past thirty years. With our
present economic organization large numbers of
intelligent, sensitive men are forced to devote their
lives to business without getting any more satisfaction out of it than Anderson did after he became successful. And, like him, these men feel the
need of other interests. The difference between
them is that Anderson with a vigorous gesture of

disdain revolted and fled the camp of "usefulness"
and respectability. He couldn't be satisfied for
long with a hobby. So real did what he was concentrating upon become to him that he must rest
convinced of its supreme and absolute importance.

The end of this, the non-literary portion of his
life, Anderson has dramatized in his autobiography, *A Story Teller's Story:* "After many years
of effort to conform to an unstated and but dimly
understood American dream by making myself a
successful man in the material world I threw all
overboard. . . . It was melodramatic and even
silly enough. . . . For several years the attempt
to sell goods had become a sort of madness with
me. . . . I was about to become rich. . . . After
a time I would build a great factory and after
that a greater and greater. Like a true American
I thought in size. . . .

"I had seen women of the streets, standing at
corners, looking furtively about. My thoughts
got fixed upon prostitution. Was I a prostitute?
Was I prostituting my life? . . . It came with a
rush, the feeling that I must quit buying and selling, the overwhelming feeling of uncleanliness. I
was in my whole nature a taleteller. The taleteller cannot bother with buying and selling. To
do so will destroy him. . . .

"I wanted to go out of the door (of the factory)
and never come back. . . . It was a trying moment for me. There was the woman, my secretary, now looking at me. What did she represent?
What did she not represent? Would I dare be

honest with her? It was quite apparent to me that I would not. I had got to my feet and we stood looking at each other. 'It is now or never,' I said to myself, and I remember that I kept smiling. I had stopped dictating to her in the midst of a sentence. 'The goods which you have inquired about are the best of their kind made in the—' I stood and she sat and we were looking at each other intently. . . .

"Whether at that moment I merely became shrewd and crafty or whether I really became temporarily insane I shall never quite know. What I did was to step very close to the woman and looking directly into her eyes I laughed gaily. I looked at my feet. 'I have been wading in a long river and my feet are wet,' I said. Again I laughed as I walked lightly toward the door and out of a long and tangled phase of my life. 'They want me to be a nut, will love to think of me as a nut, and why not? It may just be that's what I am,' I thought gaily."

He left Elyria, his family and business and went to Chicago to devote his entire attention to writing. Of course his endeavor to lead a stolid and responsible life and to find contentment and satisfaction in being an efficient cog in the American industrial machine was foredoomed to failure. For him to have stuck at it as long as he did shows what a hold on him the gospel of business success must have had.

But that he should have sought escape in writing comes as something of a surprise. For some considerable time—for just how long it is impossible to say—he had been attempting to counteract the dreariness of his life by putting down on paper thoughts, observations, imaginings. A hint as to how this habit started is found in his novel, *Many Marriages,* in which he describes a man stifled by his family and his business who leaves both to seek a more satisfying life. The book is obviously based on his own experience in Elyria. In it there is the following paragraph, which has almost no connection with the story, but which is certainly based on Anderson's personal experience:

"For a time he had read a good many books. At one time he had thought he might like to be a writer of books. And no doubt a great many of the writers of books had been visited by just such thoughts as he was having now. Within the pages of some books one found a kind of refuge from the tangle of things in daily life. Perhaps, as they wrote, these men felt, as he now felt, carried out of themselves."

In that passage there is a vague atmosphere of "culture clubs," of the belief so rife in intelligent America twenty or thirty years ago that universal education would prove a panacea for all evils, of the naïve and undiscriminating American worship —from afar—of art. Anderson, without formal education and with the instinctive respect for culture that is to be found in so many self-made men, has been reading rather widely, and in what he reads he finds many parallels to his own experi-

ence. At first tentatively, and then with growing
confidence he begins to see if he can't do something
of the same sort with his own experiences. As the
game becomes more fascinating, he devotes more
time to it, and less to his business. At the same
time that he has an almost worshipful respect for
"culture"—and a great consciousness of his own
lack of it—his typical American shrewdness and
self-confidence keep him from being abashed or
discouraged; he is intelligent; there is no reason
why he shouldn't learn the rules of this game.

In thus turning to writing as "a refuge from
the tangle of things of daily life" (and there is
ample evidence in his writing besides the passage
just quoted to prove that he did so), Anderson
was reversing the ordinary process of writers. It
is much more usual for a man who actually has
something to say to attempt to do so because he
feels the need of getting closer to life, because he
wants to work out more accurately things that he
has seen and felt in life, not because he feels the
need of a refuge from its complications. And
most good writers don't pursue their craft because
they need "to be carried out of themselves," although it often does happen that in their intent-
ness upon their task they lose all consciousness of
person. Significant writing is a heightening of
experiences and sensations, not an escape from
them.

Anderson's mental attitude when he took up
writing is of more than passing importance because of the light that it throws upon certain

qualities in his writing. In a great many of his works he devotes much space to explaining why it is that he isn't a better writer. Often these apologies are generalized so as to include other American writers; but in so doing he is really only giving the particulars of his own experience. And his experience is that of the self-made man without formal education who feels that had he been educated and "cultured" most of the difficulties would have been obviated.

Another quality of Anderson's writing which his autobiography helps to explain is the fact that so much of it is "writing of escape." We have but to recall the manner of his leaving Elyria to see how intimately the two are connected. An American business man who has made good in a remarkably few years takes up writing as a hobby, finally decides that he likes his hobby better than his business, and determines to spend the rest of his time at it. The same thing happens often enough every year in America. Life isn't so complicated that Anderson couldn't have sold his business, made what financial arrangements were possible with his wife and set out. Why was it that, in making the move, he went in for such high melodrama and felt the need to justify himself with that sentimental rhetoric about "prostituting his life"? Perhaps he had been reading too many popular lives of artists and felt called upon to start his artistic career with a flourish. But I feel that his reasons went deeper than that.

When he left Elyria, Anderson, I think, had

drugged himself into a state in which he was either unwilling or unable to distinguish between reality and fiction. For some time he had been living vicariously through the characters whom he was creating. With a clean white sheet of paper in front of him and endowed with a pleasantly romantic imagination, it was easy to make life happy and interesting for his characters. As he was living quite completely through those characters, it was much more attractive to continue to do so than to face the realities of life.

Anderson turned to writing as a refuge from life, and, having established that refuge, he retreated into it and barricaded himself there. He reënacts that retreat in almost every book he has written. He writes to escape from life and, as a rule, life escapes from his writing. It is that softness, that sentimentality, that inability or unwillingness to face things that keeps Anderson from being the great writer that he so often shows the promise of becoming. The fact that Anderson gave up his business and deserted his family because he wanted to write proves nothing. That he did so as a means of escape from reality is the all important fact.

Anderson was confused when he left Elyria. He tried to turn his back on his personal confusion and he has remained confused ever since. His experience in business left him bitter against commercialism, against the cheapness of quantity production, against the mechanics of modern life, and convinced that no good could come of the present trend of things. Anderson doesn't understand and at heart dislikes modern life. No matter that there is much in that life to dislike, it is the only life Anderson has to describe; and to do that validly, whether sympathetically or satirically, he must understand it. Unfortunately his fear-inspired dislike dulls when it does not kill his understanding. His dislike does not find utterance in a biting attack, but in the hysterical wail of a defeated man.

Forced by fate to be one of the pioneer historians of modern life, for which he has no real sympathy, Anderson is in the unfortunate position of a reactionary who is striving to be "advanced." He is "a confused child in a confused world," and much of that confusion is because in his writing, as in his life, he will not face facts. In the place of the courage which is an artist's most important possession, Anderson has an evasive sentimentality.

Anderson isn't an artist in the strict meaning of that word. He is a pleasant and engaging human being, a conscientious craftsman, an expert in the technique of writing, a skillful story teller and not a bad psychologist, but he lacks the inner hardness and determination necessary for the production of what is loosely known as art.

II. ANDERSON'S WRITINGS

WINDY McPHERSON'S SON, Sherwood Anderson's first novel, appeared in 1916, when the author was forty years old. Since then he has published one book each year with the exception of 1926, when he brought out two. That in this first book he really expressed what he wanted to say is indicated by the fact that it is difficult to find in any of the books subsequently published, with the exception of a few of his short stories, a thought or an event that is not at least hinted at in *Windy McPherson's Son*. Although he has not yet expanded them, his personal and social philosophy are substantially what they will remain for the next eleven years.

Windy McPherson was a slightly shell-shocked veteran of the Civil War who chafed under his subsequent obscure position in life and fell to loud boasting and to the nursing of a belief that not Lincoln nor Grant but he himself had thrown the winning die in the great struggle. He provided steady amusement for the Iowa farming town of Caxton and was a constant source of humiliation for his alert son Sam.

They might laugh at Windy, but Sam resolved to cherish his bargaining and money getting impulse, and to make the village sing a different tune for him. Somehow he felt that to have money would make up for the humiliations in the life of the McPherson family. "Make money! Cheat! Lie! Be one of the big men of the world! Get your name up for a modern, high-class American," advised an excited grocery-store philosopher, and Sam was inclined to follow this advice, although as yet he felt no temptation to cheat or to lie. For six years he had been Caxton's only newsboy; at the age of fifteen he sold the list of his newspaper customers and his peanut and popcorn business for three hundred and fifty dollars; in the bank seven hundred dollars were already deposited in his name. He became the buyer for a local dealer in farm products and within a year had more than doubled his employer's purchases.

"Like all boys he thought much and often of death . . . and was not without a hunger for religion," but by dint of a good deal of loud-mouthed and hypocritical evangelizing and one ghastly experience when he was called upon to make a public confession of faith, he came to dread the word soul and swore never again to enter a church. He also "discovered sex," looked at women's ankles, listened eagerly to smutty stories, looked up obscene words in the dictionary and read certain suggestive passages in the Bible. "One night when the sex call kept him awake he got up and dressed, and went and stood in the rain by the creek."

John Telfer's friendship was a formative influence in the life of Sam McPherson. The only dandy in Caxton, he had studied art in New York and Paris and talked about that, philosophy, and kindred subjects to the young newsboy. "He entered with zeal into Sam's thoughts and tried valiantly to arouse in the quiet, industrious, money-making boy some of his own love of life and beauty. At night as the two were walking down country roads, the man would stop and, waving his arms about, quote Poe or Browning or, in another mood, would compel Sam's attention to the rare smell of a hayfield or to a moonlit stretch of meadow."

This brief summary of the first section of the book is sufficient to show that Anderson is rewriting his own childhood, as he is so often to do in the future. Sam McPherson is, with obvious rearrangements of facts and emphasis, the Anderson of *A Story Teller's Story*, the Beaut McGregor of *Marching Men*, the George Willard of *Winesburg, Ohio*, and Tar in Anderson's latest novel; he also bears some resemblance to Hugh McVey in *Poor White*, to John Webster in *Many Marriages*, to Bruce Dudley in *Dark Laughter* and to characters in some of the short stories. Many other people in the book are to become more than familiar to those who follow Anderson's writings. The boastful, inefficient story-telling father; the silent, hard-working, impressive mother; the fierce, coarse Italian grandmother who knocks out a tramp when he tries to bully her; sensitive and ineffectual John Telfer; and the whole background of Caxton—to leave the list incomplete—keep returning in a series of disguises that in itself would make an interesting study.

As the book continues it gets further and further from the facts of Anderson's own life, but it keeps always closely in touch with his personal problems.

Sam goes to the city and moves from one success to another until he is an important departmental head in a world-famous company manufacturing firearms. He becomes an unmoral, hardboiled business man who is driven on by his lust for power and success. In this latter part of the book Anderson comes perilously close to the "log cabin to mansion" formula of writing. Little is said about the mature Sam that is convincing; he has become more like a puppet which Anderson uses in working out certain problems about the connection or lack of connection between business success and personal satisfaction.

Sam marries the "purposeful" daughter of the owner of the company (who rides up to meet him on a "spirited" black horse), obtains virtual control of the entire concern, and organizes a merger with similar companies all over the country that leaves him at the head of the firearms industry. Thus he becomes one of the financial giants of the world. It is all fluently enough written and Anderson works out plausible explanations of the success of his hero—but after Sam leaves Caxton he, as a character, loses his individuality and becomes largely an idea of "the big business man."

Anderson is obviously trying to work out a *reductio ad absurdum* of the American business "success" ideal. Sam breaks with his wife over a questionable business deal which she thinks unfair to her father and, not satisfied with being an American Krupp, he begins "a series of stock raids, speculations and manipulations that attracted country-wide attention. . . . They were in oil, railroads, coal, western land, mining, timber and street railways. . . . He owned running horses at the tracks, memberships in many clubs, a country house in Wisconsin and shooting preserves in Texas. He drank steadily, played poker for big stakes, kept in the public prints and day after day led his crew upon the high seas of finance. He did not dare think and in his heart he was sick of it, sick to the soul, so that when thought came to him he got out of his bed to seek roistering companions. . . . Sam was rapidly degenerating."

And thus, success turned to dust in his mouth, Sam sells out, packs his bag and disappears saying good-by to no one. "In his mind he had no definite idea of where he was going or what he was going to do. He knew only that he would follow the message his hand had written. He would spend his life seeking truth."

Anderson has made his point that a sensitive man gets no satisfaction out of being successful in business. Later, like Dreiser, Anderson will be satisfied to let his argument rest there. In *Windy McPherson's Son*, however, he follows the popular success story formula and gives a "solution" to the problem and a happy ending to the novel.

Sam stops off in a small Illinois boom town and gets a job as a carpenter. "I've been drinking and I want to work hard day after day so that my muscles may become firm and sleep come to me at night." In his search for Truth he becomes a socialist and tries to thwart a water-power grab that is being engineered by his former Chicago associates, but his identity leaks out, the towns-people suspect his motives and he leaves, disillusioned. He wanders about, attempts to aid some poor working girls on strike, runs afoul of the union and once again his philanthropic attempt comes to nothing. Evidently socialism won't solve this problem for him. "American men and women," he concludes, "have not learned to be clean and noble and natural, like their forests and their wide, clean plains."

Sam then spends a year hunting big game and another living the life of a gentleman of fashion in London, New York and Paris, and then starts drinking again, "not moderately now, but steadily and almost continuously." But even now he sometimes asks himself, "Why had I a brain and a dream and a hope? Why went I about seeking Truth?"

On one of his carouses he goes home with a woman who has attracted him and is struck by the pathetic sordidness of the lives of her three little children. He buys the children new clothes, legally adopts them and sets off for his abandoned wife, now living in seclusion in a picturesque little village on the Hudson, in whom "the mother hunger" is still alive.

In the last paragraph comes the long-awaited moral: " 'I cannot run away from life. I must face it. I must begin to try to understand these other lives, to love,' he told himself. The buried inner thing in him thrust itself up."

"Why," one wonders in closing the book, "have the usually alert movie magnates passed this up?"

Windy McPherson's Son is a bad novel and it is in no way fair to judge Sherwood Anderson's writing by it. At the same time, its very naïveté gives one a good many clews for estimating his subsequent work. Later Anderson became a superb craftsman and able by his manipulation of words to conceal many of those basic defects in his writing which are so glaring in this first novel; most of the defects, except those in craftsmanship, remained, however, despite their covering of surface gloss.

As a rule the book is most effective when it sticks to what we know to be the facts of Anderson's life. Sam's boyhood is moderately well done; incidents in it ring true, but the general tone is somewhat spoiled by the emphasis Anderson lays upon the fact that this alert, shrewd, pushing youngster is also sensitive to beauty of nature and of character and to ugliness, that he thinks about the eternal problems of existence, and that he has feelings and emotions. Anderson tries to keep these two sides to Sam's character in separate compartments, and then throws up his hands in awe as he intimates that the boy has a double personality. This habit, which one finds constantly in Anderson's writing, tends toward flatness and falsification of character. The man is yet to be born who has not two such sides to him. By keeping them so separate Anderson loses the valuable interplay of one upon the other which usually has the deciding influence upon any life. With Anderson it is either one or the other, seldom both.

It is also not unfair to complain that we are told very little by which we can actually identify Sam. He might be almost any energetic boy brought up in the Middle West, not because Anderson, as did Mark Twain, has achieved a universal quality in his description, but merely because the few and rather obvious facts we are given would apply to almost any boy in similar circumstances, regardless of his personal qualities. It is only his success, which is so romantically recounted as to be unconvincing, that differentiates Sam from his fellows.

Anderson is seldom an economical writer. He surrounds his few facts with soft and protective word-blankets. Seldom does he give enough actual information about one of the principal characters in a novel for us to recognize him were we to meet him in life. Later Anderson is to disguise this paucity of material by wordily constructed moods and atmosphere. In this novel the lack is striking.

The best done portions of the book, as in Anderson's other novels, are the quick sketches of minor characters. Several of them are short stories in themselves in which Anderson gives evidence of the manner of *Winesburg, Ohio*, his best known book and the one upon which his reputation justly rests. The best of these sketches are done with assurance, deftness and an economy that comes as a pleasant surprise in his sea of words. Without self-consciousness, or worry about philosophy or ideals, Anderson describes the phase of these people's lives that bears upon the main story, and they assume a sudden validity and individuality that the hero never achieves. John Telfer, Mary Underwood, Sam's former teacher, Windy (this is the only novel of Anderson's in which the hero's father is a convincing individual, although characters like Windy often appear) and a few of Sam's friends in later life are among those successfully characterized.

The last two-thirds of the book, which recounts Sam's career after he leaves Caxton, is so bad that the only excuse for dealing with it is Anderson's present reputation as a writer. It is sentimental romanticism of a kind the popular magazines and the movies are full of.

Anderson went into writing as an escape from life, and often his escape takes the form of wild day-dreaming on paper. He is like a poor clerk who sees in the newspapers a picture of a royal ceremony and then sits down and dreams the whole thing out with himself in the principal rôle, like a street urchin pretending to himself that he is Babe Ruth clearing the bases before a frenzied crowd. In this novel Anderson is day-dreaming about himself as a driving, clever, ruthless financial giant. It is amusing to see how seriously he takes it, how vividly he lives through the experience, but day-dreaming of that sort isn't very impressive when it is passed off as creative writing. A good deal of Anderson's writing comes into this same category.

Day-dreaming is not the only fault of the last part of the book. We also find in it an example of Anderson's most annoying defect. He is trying to make his hero work out a philosophy of life for him. When he left Elyria, Anderson was convinced of the fallacy of the "dollar ideal." Since then he has had no real philosophy (except a belief in craftsmanship), but he is constantly agitated by a suspicion that life has a meaning that has been concealed from him. He is baffled and worried about idealism, sex, beauty, truth, love, he tortures himself trying to discover what it is that man should get out of life. "I am a lover," he wails, "and I have not found my thing to love. . . . I am a confused child in a confused world." That in itself is a rather serious defect in a writer; frustrated lovers and confused children don't often see life in a wholly illuminating manner.

Anderson is quite likely to aggravate this defect by emphasizing it; he can't seem to let it alone. If he conceives a character that seems to have life and individuality, he is quite likely to put to it at once these problems that baffle him so —and naturally the characters end up in as much of a fog as he himself is in. Unfortunately in the process of trying to solve these problems, the characters cease to be characters and become confused and uninteresting ideas.

Sam McPherson is a sentimental picture of Sherwood Anderson discovering that business doesn't appeal to him. If Anderson had not given in to his desire to day-dream, and had recounted his own experience in business honestly and straightforwardly he would have produced an interesting document concerning a certain phase of the development of America. What he has actually achieved is of negligible value. The naïveté with which he sends Sam out on the search for Truth is a helpful fact to remember when, in considering his later writing, we wonder at its confusion.

Although it must be discussed at greater length further on, it is interesting to note Anderson's point of view toward America and toward life in this country. Especially significant is the passage already quoted in which he bewails the fact that American men and women "have not yet learned to be clean and noble and natural," the rather startling implication being, of course, that people elsewhere have. This feeling of Anderson's, which is self-evidently a twisted aftermath of the "Pollyanna" philosophy of life, is behind a good many of his observations. He romantically imagines that life must be so much finer in other countries and is sure that the problems of modern life are different from and more complicated than those of former generations.

It is interesting to note some of the contemporary criticisms of this first novel. The *Chicago Evening Post*, after comparing Anderson to Dreiser, Masters and Sandburg, remarks, "It is the rolling of drums. In its pages lies the promise of a new human comedy and a new, fresh, clean, and virile spirit in American literature. . . . To the end there is not a marionette present. Even those people who appear for five or ten sentences. They breathe." The *Chicago Tribune* speaks of it as "an obvious imitation of Dreiser's *The Financier*," but adds, "When Mr. Anderson doesn't try to tell a story, and merely chronicles the reaction of Sam toward life, the paragraphs are convincing." The New York papers were less awake to the new satellite in the literary heavens.

Windy McPherson's Son could be called a sociological novel; *Marching Men* comes rather definitely under that head. "Something is wrong with modern American life," says Anderson, "and we Americans do not want to look at it." As in his first novel he searched gropingly for a new set of personal ideals, here he is seeking out a new national standard of values; he is toying with the idea of finding a new slogan with which to combat the "get rich quick" battle cry. Again Anderson is after "the secret of life," but this time it is group, not individual salvation that occupies his attention.

The theme of the book is contained in the following paragraph:

"There is a curse on my country. Every one has come here for gain, to grow rich, to achieve. Suppose they should begin to want to live here. Suppose they should quit thinking of gain, leaders and followers of leaders. They are children. Suppose like children they begin to play a bigger game. Suppose they just learn to march, nothing else. Suppose they should begin to do with their bodies what their minds are not strong enough to do—just learn the one simple thing, to march, whenever two or four or a thousand of them are gathered together."

As one might guess, this book too is rather confused and inconclusive. Again Anderson is daydreaming and at the same time trying to solve the world's problems.

In general outline the plot of the two novels are distinctly alike. "Beaut" McGregor is the imaginative son of a slightly and harmlessly insane coal miner. The description of his boyhood is quite like that of Sam McPherson's. When he is about seventeen years old he resolves to break away from the bleak village in which he was born and seek fame, power and personal satisfaction in Chicago. He becomes a lawyer and almost immediately attracts national attention in a murder trial in which he sucessfully defends a criminal who has been "framed."

He is in a position to make a fortune. Instead of doing so he develops his Marching Men idea. He gets workingmen to march, peacefully and steadily, in their spare time. At first a few do it, then most of the workingmen in Chicago, and finally the movement spreads over the country.

In the midst of this he falls in love with the beautiful, talented and serious-minded daughter of a "typical" capitalist and, like Sam McPherson, his "virginal and pure power" sweeps away differences in philosophy and breeding. In a moment of self-revelation this spirited girl cries out, "I want all of life. I want the lust and the strength and the evil of it. I want to be one of the new women, the saviors of our sex." Beaut is about to marry her and give her a chance to achieve her ambitions, but he changes his mind at the last moment and returns to a devoted milliner who befriended him when he was poor and unknown. His men meanwhile have marched steadily on.

In a speech at a huge Labor Day celebration McGregor expands his philosophy:

"This talk of brotherhood. The words mean nothing. Man cannot love man. We do not know what they mean by such love. They hurt us and underpay us. . . . We have given them automobiles and wives with soft clinging dresses. When they have cried we have cared for them. . . . And now we will show them their father in his might. . . . When they see us, hundreds of thousands of us, marching into their minds and into their consciousness, then will they be afraid. And at the little meetings they have when three or four of them sit talking, daring to decide what things we shall have from life, there will be in their minds a picture. We will stamp it there. They have forgotten our power. . . . You must march shoulder to shoulder. You must march so that you yourselves shall come to know what a giant you are. . . . When you have marched until you are one giant body then will happen a miracle. A brain will grow in the giant you have made."

The relief of the reader is great when Anderson decides to dismiss his marching men with the promise of a miracle at some undecided date in the future. His philosophy was becoming so confused that it might easily have taken several more volumes to give it any semblance of coherence. He ends where he starts, greatly impressed with the potential power of labor and with the difficulty of organizing and directing it. In completing the circle he has made a great many unenlightening remarks about life. One closes the book deeply convinced that Anderson is neither a sociologist nor a philosopher.

There are short episodes scattered through the book which remind us that Anderson can write much better than this, but most of the attempted characterization and description are invalidated by the author's preoccupation with sociology. Again he has abused his characters by making them embodiments of confused ideas.

Later, in *A Story Teller's Story*, Anderson

wrote, "The magazines were filled with these plot stories and most of the plays on our stage were plot plays. 'The Poison Plot,' I called it in conversation with my friends as the plot notion did seem to me to poison all story telling. . . . The plots were frameworks about which the stories were to be constructed and editors were inordinately fond of them. One got 'an idea for a story.' What was meant was that a new trick had been thought out." After reading these first two novels one agrees heartily with him in decrying stories built about "ideas." Would that he had felt that antipathy earlier in his career!

WINESBURG, OHIO

When we come to Anderson's first volume of short stories we find ourselves far from the "poison plot." The sentimental day-dreamer and mystified philosopher are tucked away in the background and in their place is a patient, competent, sympathetic writer trying honestly and with marked penetration to record certain phenomena that he has observed.

Winesburg, Ohio is a psychological document of the first importance; no matter that it is an incomplete picture of modern American life, it is an honest and penetrating one done with bold and simple strokes. These stories represent the finest combination Anderson has yet achieved of imagination, intuition and observation welded into a dramatic unity by painstaking craftsmanship.

They are one of the important products of the American literary renascence and have probably influenced writing in America more than any book published within the last decade. They made and they sustain Anderson's reputation as an author worthy of comparison with the great short story writers.

It is in no way surprising that Anderson should find his most complete expression in the short story. His very approach to writing leads one to expect it. "I have come," he writes, "to think that the true history of life is but a history of moments. It is only at rare moments that we live." This often reiterated belief of his that only moments of "awareness" are important is much more conducive to the episodic treatment of the short story than to the cumulative continuity of the novel.

Not only does Anderson look at life from the short story point of view, but this medium tends naturally to restrain and to correct what we have already seen to be two of the great weaknesses in his writing. In such limited space there is little chance for him to become tangled up in profitless philosophic speculations; as a result of being forced to concentrate and focus his attention, Anderson forgets somewhat his worries about ultimate values and devotes himself to the definite and factual present, to the great profit of his writing. The short story also offers fewer temptations to day-dreaming, which may be indulged in more pleasantly in the more leisurely form of the novel.

The first thing to strike one in reading these stories is Anderson's extraordinary technical brilliance. The clumsiness and obvious attempts to imitate various writers which were so noticeable in the first two novels are lacking. Anderson tells these stories with a simplicity and a sureness that show that at last he knows what he is doing and how he wants to do it. He has his medium in such complete control that it is not difficult to be unconscious of his mastery of it. His air of simplicity and ingenuousness, the apparent rambling, the way in which he appears to be haphazardly setting down ideas as they come into his mind in an attempt to discover their meaning, his groping, his artlessness, his naïveté—these are but tricks of the story teller's trade to earn our sympathy for the story which he unfolds graphically and without confusion. To be sure, that groping naïveté betokens a certain self-consciousness on the part of the author, but such self-consciousness is an integral part of Anderson, and rarely does it become obtrusive.

It is in their objectiveness, in their penetration into and interpretation of universal human qualities that these stories differ from most of Anderson's writing. The important creative imaginations have always been interpretive, they have allowed their possessors to get under the surface, to understand life as it is. Thus in this broader sense all valid writing is realistic, whether the approach of the individual writer be allegorical, lyrical, symbolic, or whether it be through the more

limited realism of a Zola. Distorting life, recon-
structing it as a writer thinks it should be, writing
with any view in mind except that of interpreting
what is and what has always been is, despite popular misconceptions, not to write with imagination,
but without it. Much of Anderson's writing be-
longs to this latter class. In *Winesburg, Ohio*,
however, and in a few of his other short stories he
shows that he can penetrate objectively into the
confused world of emotion and bring back from it
at least a part of what he has seen and felt there.

What Anderson is seeking to express in these
stories is the intricacy and subtlety that exists in
the relationship of an individual to his physical
environment and to other people. He is study-
ing the means by which this relationship is established, how it is expressed, the use and the insuffi-
ciency of words in expressing it, the effect upon
the individual of his failure to establish such re-
lationships. In exploring this field Anderson in-
cidentally shows the loneliness, the essential isola-
tion of all people, however far they may or may
not have gone toward orienting themselves in
life.

The universality of the emotions Anderson describes is, paradoxically enough, far greater than
that of the characters whom he has chosen to be
the instruments through which these emotions are
depicted. It would be difficult to find another
book in which there is such a weird collection of
eccentrics, perverts, maniacs, half-wits, frustrated,
hopelessly confused people. In running quickly

through the twenty-four stories, we meet the following depressing individuals: Wing Biddlebaum whose quick, expressive hands are never in repose. He is one of those perfect school-teachers "who rule by a power so gentle that it passes as a lovable weakness. . . . Here and there went his hands, caressing the shoulders of the boys, playing about the tousled heads. . . . A half-witted pupil imagined unspeakable things and in the morning went forth to tell his dreams as facts. Strange, hideous accusations fell from his loose-hung lips." During the night a dozen men drive Wing from town; they are going to hang him, but relent. Wing never again dares have any contact with his fellows.

Continuing hurriedly we find that an hysterical pregnant girl marries the gnarled old doctor who fills his pockets with thoughts jotted down on bits of paper and rolled into hard little balls. Then follow: The morbid, eccentric philosopher who is trying to write a book to prove that every one in the world is Christ and that they are all crucified. The nervous, frightened young newspaper reporter, not sure whether he is seducing or being seduced by a laborer's daughter. Jesse Bentley, a would-be minister, who becomes instead a driving prosperous farmer; as a result of pondering over the patriarchs of the Bible he conceives the idea of sacrificing his beloved grandson, whom he has symbolically caused to be named David. Alice Hindman who broods over the memory of her forgetful fiancé for ten years and finally in an outburst of suppressed eroticism dashes naked out into the rain.

After this comes the ghastly story of Wash Williams who sent his wife back to her mother when he discovered that she had three lovers. He could never abide the sight of a woman after his final experience when he went to forgive his wife and bring her home. Her scheming mother kept Wash waiting two hours and then sent her in to him entirely naked. After Wash, we meet: The Reverend Curtis Hartman who plays Peeping Tom for several weeks until the naked, cigarette-smoking woman upon whom he is spying suddenly throws herself upon her knees and begins to pray fervently. The school teacher, Kate Swift, who thinks she is interested in the writing of one of her pupils but discovers that instead she wants him to make love to her. Belle Carpenter who out of pique at her fiancé tries to seduce a young boy.

Harping still upon sex, Anderson presents: Ray Pearson, the oppressed husband who struggles to tell his friend that if he marries the girl whom he has "got into trouble" he will be tied to a treadmill for the rest of his life. Young Tom Foster who becomes oppressed by the sordidness of sex when he is working as a Western Union messenger in the red light district of Cincinnati. He gets drunk to dissipate his growing fondness for the banker's daughter. The worn-out hotel keeper's wife who feels human sympathy for the first time when, just before her death, her doctor listens patiently to the story of her life and quiets her with passionate kisses. The adolescent boy and girl who feel the seriousness of their approaching maturity so keenly that their kisses and fondling seem tame by comparison.

Of the eight stories not included in this brief sketch, two, the first in the book and the last, serve as prologue and epilogue. Two take up the difficulty a mother has in understanding her son and in expressing her love for him. One is a romantic trifle about a little girl who "wants to be Tandy." The other three are the sad histories of eccentrics who can't possibly fit into the ordinary scheme of life.

Anderson has peopled his mythical Winesburg with strikingly abnormal types; often he goes still further and selects as the basis for his story abnormal events in their lives. It is true that there are such people in most communities and that such events as he pictures do occur; but they are exceptions, not the rule. Anderson would probably be the last to claim that this volume represents a cross section of any American town or village. He has consciously neglected the normal in favor of the sub- or abnormal. But, and in this is the genius of the book, in the neglected "normal" majority there are usually the germs that, unresisted, have caused the abnormality in the people Anderson describes. Those people about whom he does not write are normal because their processes of resistance and of adaptation have made them so.

Thus the universality of *Winesburg, Ohio* does

not depend upon the frequency with which such
types as it describes occur in the world. It goes
deeper than that. The emotions and reactions it
exposes belong, in varying degrees, to all people.
Anderson has dramatized them and made them
obvious. He has simplified, focused his attention;
in so doing he has produced grotesque people, but
they are validly, fundamentally alive people, such
as it is the fortune of comparatively few writers
to achieve. He has had to sacrifice much to ob-
tain the desired result, but the important thing is
that he has obtained it. Most of the stories ring
true, even if in a minor key.

Anderson has been widely criticized for the
sordidness of *Winesburg;* he has been called igno-
rant, perverted, immoral; even his friend, Paul
Rosenfeld, termed him "the Phallic Chekhov."
And there can be no question that he has chosen
unpleasant subjects and that he is greatly preoccupied with sex. More than two-thirds of the
stories have definitely sexual themes. This is
partly due to the influence upon him of D. H.
Lawrence and of the psychoanalysts, but even
more it is because, using sex as a point of depar-
ture, he is able to depict emotions and reactions
that are true not only of sex, but of almost all
other human relations. It is for this reason that
we close a book dealing so largely with sexual
problems, not conscious so much of its sexual nature as of the way in which it has exposed the
difficulty which the individual experiences in

orienting himself in regard to his environment and to the people around him.

Just as the emotions these characters have are more significant than the characters themselves, so these "sexual crises" have implications much wider than those of mere sex. In most of the stories the climax throws light not so much upon the sexual nature of the characters concerned as upon their general emotional make-up. A similar thing might have happened in a realm quite disassociated from sex. Whatever his reason for so doing, Anderson has used sexual examples. To do this constantly is, to my mind, a decided weakness in craftsmanship; it in no important way invalidates the integrity of the conception of the stories. We may question Anderson's taste in concentrating so much upon sex; we cannot question his right to do so. Creative writing cannot be limited by the fickle demands of "good taste."

It is easy enough to pick out flaws in *Winesburg, Ohio*. Anderson has lost immeasurably in convincingness by the necessity he has felt himself under to dramatize these stories so highly; he makes his points, but he has to do it by the sledge-hammer method. One longs for a touch of delicacy or restraint. Occasionally the stories call to mind the lists of "awful examples" sent out by welfare organizations, the anti-saloon and anti-cigarette leagues. One also longs for a single fully-rounded character; what Anderson says about these people is true, but it isn't all the

truth; there are important phases of their existence about which he seems to know nothing. This
comes partly from the over-dramatization and
partly from his theory of life as a history of moments. He sometimes neglects important influences
that have brought about these moments. It is this
lack of roundness, of completeness that must force
us to list *Winesburg, Ohio* among the minor, if
authentic, literary achievements.

OTHER SHORT STORIES

In *The Triumph of the Egg* and *Horses and
Men* there are isolated stories that rank with the
best of Anderson's work, but neither of these books
has the sustained quality of *Winesburg, Ohio*. In
tone, both are more pleasant. Anderson is no
longer entirely preoccupied with sex and suppression. In fact in one story when a character
cries out, "Sex. It is by understanding sex I will
untangle the mystery (of life)," Anderson, to
our astonishment, comments, "It was all very well
and sometimes interesting but one grew tired of
the subject."

Three of the most successful stories in these two
volumes have to do with horse racing, of which
the best is, *I Want to Know Why*. It is told in
the first person by a young boy who has run away
from home to follow the horses:

"If you've never been crazy about thorough-
breds it's because you've never been around where
they are much and don't know any better.

They're beautiful. There isn't anything so lovely and clean and full of spunk and honest and everything as some race horses. . . . It brings a lump to my throat when a horse runs. I don't mean all horses but some. I can pick them nearly every time. Even when they just go slop-jogging along with a little nigger on their backs I can tell a winner. If my throat hurts and it's hard for me to swallow, that's him. He'll run like Sam Hill when you let him out. . . .

"On Wednesday the big Mulford handicap was to be run. Middlestride was in it and Sunstreak. . . . What had happened was that both these horses are the kind it makes my throat hurt to see. Middlestride is long and looks awkward and is a gelding . . . and if the race is a mile and a quarter he'll just eat up everything and get there. Sunstreak is different. . . . It makes you ache to see him. It hurts you. He just lays down and runs like a bird dog. There can't anything I ever see run like him except Middlestride when he gets untracked and stretches himself. . . .

"Before the race I went over to the paddocks to see, I looked a last look at Middlestride, who isn't such a much standing in a paddock that way, then I went to see Sunstreak. It was his day. I knew when I saw him. . . . In some way, I can't tell just how, I knew just how Sunstreak felt inside. He was quiet and letting the niggers rub his legs and Mr. Van Riddle himself put the saddle on, but he was just like a raging torrent inside. . . . Sunstreak ran first, of course, and he busted the world's record for a mile. I've seen that if I never see anything more."

There is real quality in that story. Its fumbling inarticulateness is eloquent beyond the power of mere words to convey meaning. It is impossible ever to forget that boy standing in front of the race horse with his throat hurting. In it there is somewhat the same lyric note that one gets in Keats' *Ode to a Nightingale*. Anderson recaptures the same emotion, less successfully, in the stories, *I'm a Fool* and *An Ohio Pagan*. But having mentioned Keats, I must hasten to add that Anderson remains at that height but for a fleeting moment. *I Want to Know Why* ends in an anticlimax so banal as to make one wonder whether it wasn't by pure chance that Anderson caught the lyric note at all. He concludes what might have been a perfect story by expressing a bewildered astonishment that life can be so lovely and so sordid at the same time; the poet has been replaced by the quack philosopher.

The following rough outline will suffice to give a general idea of the other stories in the two books that are worth attention.

Seeds. The story of a lonely girl from Iowa who comes to the city to find love and companionship but can never break down the barrier between herself and other people.

The Egg. A lumbering humorous account of the hazards of chicken farming and of the vacillating hatred of a boy for his ineffectual father.

Unlighted Lamps. A country doctor marries

an actress and is unable to express his love for her. "How his hands ached to reach out across the narrow space that separated them and touch her hands, her face, her hair." But he doesn't and she gets tired of life in the small town and goes back to the stage. After which the doctor has the same difficulty establishing an intimate relationship with his daughter, and dies of heart failure just as he has made up his mind, after twenty years, to "warm up to her."

The Man in the Brown Coat. A man finds it impossible to establish personal relations with his wife. "We sit together in the evening but I do not know her. I cannot shake myself out of myself. My wife is very gentle and she speaks softly but she cannot come out of herself."

The Door of the Trap. A college professor marries and has three children. Married life is a prison to both husband and wife. There is not as much mutual understanding between them as between each of them and the negro servant. The professor becomes enamored of a young pupil who comes frequently to the house and who represents to him unimprisoned youth. He kisses her passionately one night and asks her never to return to the house.

The New Englander. Elsie Leander is a middle-aged prim New England old maid who moves to the Middle West and is prompted to an outburst of frustrated eroticism by the sight of a boy and a girl kissing.

Motherhood. A young farmer and a country

lass meet surreptitiously. "He plowed her deeply.
He planted the seeds of a young son in the warm,
rich, quivering soil."

Out of Nowhere into Nothing. Rosalind Wes-
cott comes home to a little Iowa village to discuss
with her mother her impending love affair with her
married employer, but finds herself unable to talk
to her mother or to any one else. She has grown
out of all sympathy with the village; no one there
could ever, she feels, "break through the walls of
themselves to the white wonder of life." She finds,
unexpectedly, that living next door is a man who
understands all that is happening to her, a man
with much broader sympathies than any one she
has known in Chicago. Out of that sympathy she
gains the courage to tell her mother what she is
contemplating, and departs once more for the city.

I'm a Fool. A boy who has worked around
race horses and who has a dead sure tip, dresses
up in "dude" clothes and sits in the grandstand
to watch the races. He gets into conversation
with a girl with whom he is instantly smitten;
gives her his tip, on which she wins heavily; and
tells her a long story about his father being a
very rich man and the owner of well known race
horses. Later, because of his lying about himself,
he can't see or get in touch with the girl again.

Unused. The youngest sister in a family in
which the other girls have "gone on the town"
shows her individuality by taking scholastic hon-
ors in the high school and making the village ac-
cept her as "a nice girl." Finally she too is se-

duced and at once the community remarks that "blood will tell." After a few useless attempts to regain favor she commits suicide.

The Sad Horn Blowers. An autobiographical episode which Anderson later treats more effectively in *A Story Teller's Story.*

An Ohio Pagan. Tom Edwards, a lad of sixteen, is one of the two people who can handle an ugly-tempered trotting horse named Bucephalus. Stepping into the sulky at the last moment, he drives the horse to victory in an important race at Columbus. He becomes famous and is envied by all his companions. The truant officer then threatens his employer with jail if Tom doesn't go back to school. The boy runs away, grows philosophical and wonders a good deal about God, women and education.

Of these eleven stories all, with the possible exception of the last, deal directly with the "walls" that separate individuals from each other, with the desire that people have for intimacy and the practical impossibility of their achieving it. It is almost as if Anderson were retelling the same story and merely applying it to different people each time. The lonely young Middle Western old maid, the ineffectual farmer, the country doctor, the writer, the college professor, the prim New England old maid, the young farmer, the intelligent private secretary, the race track swipe, the bright daughter in a degenerate family, all have practically the same difficulty in adjusting themselves to life, the same kind of longings and dissatisfactions. It is merely that the effect of these things on them differs according to the peculiarities of the individual.

These stories are decidedly more mature, less naïve than those in *Winesburg;* technically they are handled better; Anderson hasn't warped and twisted his characters as he did in that first volume of short stories. The characters are no longer such striking gargoyles and grotesques.

But in thus restraining himself, Anderson has lost immeasurably in vividness, convincingness and in what he himself terms "truth to the essence of things." The exteriors of these people are more recognizable; what happens to them is less so. Whatever one's reaction to *Winesburg,* one could scarcely feel that it was dull or commonplace. One often feels that about these stories. Was not the technique of their telling so well handled, it would be virtually impossible to read many of them. One feels that Anderson is running a little dry; he is having to skimp and to squeeze on his emotions. In *Winesburg* one felt that he was writing because he actually had something to say; in most of these stories one wonders if he isn't writing merely because he wants to write and knows how it should be done.

LATER NOVELS

Anderson has so far published five novels; in addition to the two already discussed, there are *Poor White, Many Marriages,* and *Dark Laugh-*

ter. They are not good novels; not one of them, considered as a whole, compares with his better short stories. Yet they all contain episodes that are almost short stories in themselves and that, as episodes, hold their own with anything he has written.

Each of these novels wobbles annoyingly toward the end; in each one the hero's character, which is usually fairly convincing at the beginning, becomes more and more confused as the book progresses. In each of them there are several minor characters more convincing than those to whom the author devotes most of his attention. Each is at its worst when it deals with sex and idealism. Each contains to some degree what we have seen to have been the two outstanding weaknesses of his first novels: a preoccupation with "the meaning of life" that leads him to put his personal problems to characters in a book, and an inclination to tell himself fairy stories about life instead of going through the hard work of actually understanding and expressing it. And each is written with a mastery of technique that is at times amazing.

It may be instructive to enquire briefly into some of the possible reasons for Anderson's shortcomings as a novelist. It would be easy to blame most of them on his theory that the true history of life is a history of moments—and by moments, Anderson means, of course, climactic moments— did not the flaw go deeper, were it not that his very way of looking at life, his comprehension of it force him to adopt this theory. If Anderson were a great writer, if he were able to grasp all of the important causes of these "moments" and to deduce all the significant results from them, his theory would work quite as well in a novel as in a short story. But he does not possess that gift. In a book like *Winesburg, Ohio*, for instance, he showed that he knew pretty well what was happening at a given "moment." Even in that book, however, there was little comprehension of what went on before and what followed. A novel almost always moves from one "moment" to another. If they do not flow naturally one into another, if they are not combined and related, the novel, instead of gaining in effectiveness as it proceeds, loses it. This is what happens to Anderson's novels. The really effective episodes are rarely those which bear directly on the main story; much more often they are detached vignettes, sketches of minor characters, "colorful" episodes inserted to establish a desired atmosphere.

Thus it is fair to say that one of the chief troubles with Anderson's writing, if indeed it be not the principal one, is his lack of actual knowledge of his characters. This failing he disguises at once. He has a vivid imagination of the type possessed by children who tell each other stories. When his interpretive imagination fails him and he lacks actual facts, he falls back upon this childish imagination. He makes up stories about characters and situations that "will do just as well," and when he does that, instead of "being true to the essence of things," he reconstructs events as he would like them to have been. He has an innate feeling that life is wrong and when he falls back upon this childish imagination, he remakes it as he feels it should be—which is essentially the method of the "Pollyanna" school of writing which he so detests. True writing consists in heightening life, not in disguising it.

In the foreword to *Tar*, Anderson admits his failing and tries to excuse it. "All tale telling," he writes, "is, in a strict sense, nothing but lying. This is what people cannot understand. To tell the truth is too difficult. I long since gave up the effort." Real writing is not lying, as Anderson himself proved in *Winesburg, Ohio* and in passages in his other books. Neither is it too difficult to tell the truth when one is conscious of a truth to be told, as Anderson is at times. It is only when he has nothing to say that Anderson descends to lying.

Before continuing our discussion of these novels, it is necessary to note in passing one legend which has grown up about Anderson and which he himself has done a great deal to spread. It is the picture of a dynamic man who sees all, feels all, and understands all but is kept from telling what he knows by his insuperable inarticulateness. It is the picture of a clumsy, uneducated man groping for words with which to express himself. The image is highly fallacious. Few American writers have had the sheer virtuosity, the fluency, the control over words that Anderson possesses. He can put words together so well that he can say nothing for pages on end and still entice on even a reluctant reader; there comes, of course, an aftermath of resentment at being thus deluded, but Anderson reduces it to a minimum by cannily distracting the reader's attention from what has happened by awakening new hopes for the future, and by subtly arousing in his mind a question as to whether he actually understood all that the author had to say.

When Anderson has something to say he says it, and says it effectively. What he is groping so painfully for is for something to say. Despite his varied experience in early life, the number of things about which he writes is strictly limited. Most of the important events in his own life he has described from three to half a dozen times. Anderson has devoted himself to writing as people of old devoted themselves to the crafts. He has learned every trick of the story teller's trade. Writing has given him a refuge from "the tangle of things of daily life"; it has provided him with an extensive outlet for his restless and dramatic imagination and a chance to practice the craftsmanship that he has come to think of as the only road to personal satisfaction. But, and perhaps in this lies Anderson's great tragedy, he lacks the raw material with which to pursue his craft. He must skimp and be niggardly. Having constructed, he must tear down and re-use the material. The paucity of his material is not so noticeable in the limited space of a short story; in a

novel it becomes striking. And when, thus handi-
capped, he holds religiously to the production of
at least one volume each year, his failing becomes
somewhat a matter for public concern.

In his third novel, as in his first two, Anderson
tells the story, so dear to American ears, of the
penniless country lad who makes a fortune—and
as before he adds his own little moral to the effect
that money and the power that go with it don't
make a man happy. But *Poor White*, despite its
plot, has more to recommend it than had Anderson's first two novels. It contains, for one thing, a
fine description of the transition of a Middle
Western town from a small farming community
to a thriving industrial center, and in it there
are also some valid observations as to the effect
of that change on various individuals. A few
of the sketches of minor characters almost reach
the plane Anderson achieved in *Winesburg, Ohio*,
but the hero and heroine are insipid puppets.

Hugh McVey is represented as being a listless
and anemic descendant of Huck Finn, who lives in
the Missouri village of Mudcat Landing, on the
Mississippi. He comes under the influence of a
sharp-tongued, thrifty, energetic New England
woman, who "with all her mother's soul wanted
to protect Hugh." He is unbelievably lazy and
shiftless by nature, but so strong is the woman's
influence upon him that, when he leaves her care
and is working as a section hand in another town,
he never allows himself a moment of repose for

fear of becoming a loafer again. He would sometimes, we are told, spend most of the night going
through the town counting the pickets in the
fences in front of the houses. After which he
would estimate the number of pickets that could be
cut out of an ordinary-sized tree; and then how
many could be cut from all the trees in town.
Later, if there were time, he would snatch a few
hours' sleep and start for work.

Anderson often verges on the ridiculous in his
description of Hugh and occasionally he achieves
it.

As a result of his fear of doing nothing, Hugh
masters the intricacies of applied mechanics (the
correspondence schools lending the author a help-
ing hand), and becomes an inventor. He invents
machines for planting cabbages, for loading hay,
for dumping loaded freight cars into the holds of
ships and becomes rich and famous.

He marries the daughter of a rich farmer and
industrial promoter. His wife has been to college, has thought a good deal about the place of
"modern woman" in the world, but hasn't solved
many problems. On the bridal evening Hugh
sneaks out of the bedroom when his new wife isn't
looking, muttering, "I won't let her do it," and
wanders around the fields all night. It isn't until
a week later that he musters the nerve to con-
summate the marriage. The book ends on a hope-
ful but confused note with the passing of Clara,
the college graduate, into the background. "At
that moment the woman who had been a thinker

stopped thinking. Within her arose the mother,
fierce, indomitable, strong with the strength of the
roots of a tree." One wonders a bit whether that
is Anderson's advice to all women, or whether it
merely works in Clara's case. One is not even
convinced that Clara will get so far just because
she stops thinking. Perhaps Anderson got tired.

The main points of the story do not come much
closer to ringing true than most conventional "log
cabin to mansion" stories, or the blurb of a press
agent about a famous inventor. There are a few
pages in the novel, however, in which Anderson
catches admirably the thrill, the excitement, the
exuberant heedless optimism that ran through the
country with the coming of factories.

There is an admirable portrait of Joe Wains-
worth, the harness maker: "I know my trade and
do not have to bow down to any man. . . . Learn
your trade. Don't listen to talk. The man who
knows his trade is a man. He can tell every one
to go to the devil." Joe, of course, is pushed to
the wall by machine-made goods. Anderson
greatly injures the portrait at the end by a
flagrantly over-dramatic episode wherein Joe mur-
ders his assistant. Jim, a farm hand, Tom But-
terworth, the rich farmer and promoter, and
Steve Hunter, "an early Rotarian," are also convincingly sketched.

In *Poor White* Anderson's day-dreaming qualities are most in evidence; in *Many Marriages* his
worry about "problems" runs away with him.

Many Marriages is a good example of what is
often spoken of as Anderson's "mysticism." It
is not real mysticism at all, but mystification. It
is Anderson's old search for "the meaning of life"
dramatized, sentimentalized, disguised in a soft
mush of words with a little unsuccessful symbol-
ism thrown in for flavoring. In his first novels
Anderson came right out with his problems and his
attempted solutions; it was direct and vigorous, if
unsuccessful. There is a whining, insinuating
note in *Many Marriages* that becomes increasingly
annoying. The book is filled with prose poems
that don't come off, with endless petty yearnings
and complaints. Anderson has stretched out the
material for a mediocre short story into a full
length novel and has made the material itself
worthless in the process. The book rambles; re-
peats words, thoughts, symbols; were it not so
thoroughly confused and meaningless, it would
come very close to being immoral.

There are four characters: John Webster, a
middle-aged manufacturer, who feels that he isn't
getting what he should out of life; Mrs. Webster,
a dumpy useless woman without a trace of emotional or intellectual life; Jane Webster, the
daughter, without convictions, emotions or ideas,
who will turn out to be like her mother but whom
John Webster thinks he can "save"; Natalie
Schwartz, the stenographer who placidly accepts
her employer's love. Except for John Webster,
none of the other characters ever achieve any
semblance of life. The plot is simple. Webster

decides to desert his wife and his business and to go off with his stenographer, with whom he falls in love because she is the only other woman he sees. Before leaving he wants to explain his action to his daughter.

Anderson feels vaguely that there is something noble in the man's action; but at the end of the book, after two hundred and fifty pages of listening to the workings of Webster's mind, when he and Natalie Schwartz walk out into the night and Mrs. Webster commits suicide, the reader has a distinct impression that Webster hasn't made a very noble gesture, that he hasn't made much progress toward solving his problems, and that within a few weeks he will wish desperately that he could run back to his home, his wife and his business.

The whole book works up to the climactic scene where Webster arranges an altar in his bedroom, with candles, a crucifix and a painting of the Madonna. He then undresses and struts before this altar in what Anderson would have us believe an ecstasy of cleanliness and regeneration. The pot-bellied, be-spectacled little man has become a mystic! . . .

The last hundred and fifty pages of the book might easily be disgusting were they not ridiculous. Naked before this altar, Webster tells his daughter, who is clad in a thin nightgown, what he thinks about life and love, and from time to time he half makes love to her himself.

Many Marriages is Anderson run completely

amuck. It is a painful book to read, for the author is obviously striving to be honest and sincere; he is writing with the utmost seriousness and is trying to portray the intangible, subtle nuances of life. The harder he tries, the more ridiculous the story becomes.

At the bottom of *Many Marriages* is an incurably romantic and sentimental outlook on life. Anderson is trying to read into life things that aren't there at all, or, perhaps better, which aren't at all where he thinks they are.

In *Dark Laughter* we have a new Anderson; he is restrained, mellow, observant; no longer does he torture himself about "the meaning of life"; nor does he remake it. He is writing autobiographically, but he maintains a certain objectiveness and detachment; he rearranges facts, but in the process does not destroy them. Never before or since has he handled a hero so well; he still holds to his "moments" theory, but the moments are so coördinated and related that one flows naturally into another. Bruce Dudley is substantially the same man in all parts of the book—which is more than can be said for the heroes of the other novels. When Anderson is sentimental it is with moderation; it does not upset all balance of values; indeed it lends a tone of mellowness to his writing. It is true that the novel weakens toward the end, but it is the first novel in which Anderson is able to reach the final page without collapsing. Technically it is one of his most brilliant performances; for the first time he is master of the intricacies of the novel.

Dark Laughter is easily Anderson's best novel, but seldom does it rise above the level of the second rate. It is good, skillful, perceptive writing, much better than the average "competent" novel, but still not very exciting when compared to the best of this or of other ages. Anderson has overcome a good many of his faults but in so doing he has dissipated a number of his positive virtues. The book shows very plainly the influence, either direct or indirect, of such writers as Joyce and Proust; and it is feeble compared to the work of either of them.

It is possible that in *Dark Laughter* Anderson is attempting to work out, from an entirely different point of view, what he tried so unsuccessfully to do in *Many Marriages*. Bruce Dudley, like John Webster, gets fed up with his job and his wife and decides to leave them both. Starting from Chicago, he drifts down the Mississippi to New Orleans, loafs about for a while, returns to the Indiana town where he was born, works in an automobile factory and later as a gardener, falls in love with his employer's wife and runs away with her before the bewildered husband's eyes. Except for the final elopement, which is in the nature of a dramatic after-thought dragged in to provide the conventional climax, the book runs a steady, compelling, impressive course.

Gone are the fake mysticism and hysterical sentimentality. When Bruce Dudley leaves his wife

he merely walks out the door; neither he nor she
have any deep feeling about it.   Anderson has
shown convincingly that their married life had become a not very satisfactory economic arrange-
ment, unsupported by emotional or intellectual
sympathy.   They lived together, but except for
half-hearted quarrels they had no relations that
were not formal and essentially meaningless.
Bruce was a tired, superficially cynical newspaper
reporter who didn't want commercial success.   His
wife was a clever hack writer who was destined
before long to become highly successful.   She
was pushing and energetic; he lazy and desirous
of taking things easy; he had a nebulous desire to
write but didn't let it worry him.

His guiding philosophy was that "when things
got settled you were through, might as well sit in
a rocking chair waiting for death.   Death, before
life came."   He dreaded becoming the type of
man who "wanted a nice, firm little wall built
around him, who wanted to be safe behind the wall,
feel safe.   A man within the walls of a house, safe,
a woman's hand holding his hand, warmly—await-
ing him.   All others shut out by the walls of the
house."

Bruce, drifting down the Mississippi in a row-
boat, lying naked on a bed on a hot New Orleans
night listening to the laughter and songs of the
niggers, painting wheels in an automobile factory,
unhurried, undisturbed, loafing, thinking when
thoughts come to him but not seeking them, content merely to enjoy the simple acts and sights of

life without worry about past or future, reminiscing and day-dreaming Bruce is a more lacka-
daisical Huck Finn grown up and returned to his
old haunts. At times Anderson makes Bruce out
to be the content, irresponsible wanderer that
every man at some time or other dreams of becoming.

The story is a thoroughly Proustian psychological monologue.; Bruce, working in the automobile factory, is reminiscing to himself, and
through his wandering thoughts we get his life as
he has seen it. The tempo of the story is admirably controlled; never does the monologue become
unintentionally monotonous; soliloquies, psychological analyses, descriptions, lyric moments, anecdotes are woven into a lively and harmonious
pattern. At times apparently confused, the total
effect of the story is one of great simplicity and
cohesion.

There are, however, a number of technical defects. After the manner of James Joyce and
Virginia Woolf, Anderson sometimes attempts to
achieve the effect of recurrent ideas in a man's
mind by repeating thoughts, words and phrases in
a sort of refrain; but he fails to attain the desired
result and leaves us instead conscious of the poverty and lack of variety of his material. Also the
dialogue, as in most of his books, is abominable.
The characters speak more often in Anderson's
own idiom than in their own. As has already been
remarked, toward the end of the book Anderson
falls back into the melodramatic faults of his early

novels, but even so, *Dark Laughter* is for him a tremendous step forward.

Early in the novel we are given Anderson's definition of art, at which no one could quibble: "Art is something out beyond reality, a fragrance touching the reality of things through the fingers of a humble man filled with love." It is only unfortunate that, necessary as they are, humility and love are not the only qualities requisite for the production of art.

AUTOBIOGRAPHY AND ESSAYS

If one really wants to know Sherwood Anderson, the writer, it is only necessary to turn to *A Story Teller's Story;* there one finds Anderson, all of Anderson that gets into his books, and a good deal of the man behind the books. In *A Story Teller's Story* Anderson is yarning, yarning about what he has done, where he has been, what he has seen, about people he has met and observations he has made. Some of it actually happened, some of it didn't, but it is all Sherwood Anderson.

It is a rambling, informal collection of reminiscences, essays, imaginings; it contains character sketches that rank with Anderson's better works, autobiographical anecdotes that have obviously served as the bases for much of his writing, observations upon life and manners in America of which some are confused and insipid and others so vivid, spontaneous and accurate that they take one's breath away. One gets the impression that

Anderson, forgetful of art, unself-conscious for
once, is merely sitting down to tell a succession
of interesting stories confident that his audience
isn't bored. Perhaps it is not quite exact to say
that he is unself-conscious; Anderson never for a
moment forgets his audience; he is watching it,
playing with it, experimenting. But his self-
consciousness is that of an actor rather than of a
man unsure of himself.

The volume is divided into four books. The
first deals with his boyhood, the same boyhood
that he has so often described in his other works.
The poor family living in haunted houses to escape
paying rent, three boys sleeping in a single bed
to save bedclothes, the silent impressive mother
and the talkative, story-telling vagrant father.
Although he manages to describe the atmosphere
in which he grew up, most of the hundred and
thirty pages of the first book are devoted to the
telling of two stories: one supposedly by his
father, "Major" Anderson, in which various romantic episodes in the Civil War are revised and
described; the other by Sherwood himself when
he is lying buried in the hay in a farmer's barn
telling himself about smugglers and South American revolutionists with fierce cruel eyes, bronze
complexions and black mustaches. These stories
are unalloyed sentimental romances of a Saturday
Evening Post or Cosmopolitan Magazine type.
But they pretend to be nothing else, and as such
they are amusing interludes.

The second book is largely composed of anec-

dotes about his life during the years spent wandering around the country immediately after leaving
home when his mother died. He works with race
horses, in a bicycle factory, rolls kegs of nails out
of.a warehouse and loads them on trucks, remi-
nisces about his boyhood, fights with a fellow
workman and tries to bluff his chambermaid into
believing that he won the fight, saves money for
drinking and reading bouts, and finally enlists for
the Spanish American war to avoid returning to
a factory. He includes several good character
sketches among the rambling anecdotes.

The third book contains the description, already quoted, of Anderson's leaving his wife and
business in Elyria; a statement of his philosophy
as a writer; a lyric bit about the joys of sitting
before a piece of white paper, as yet untouched by
a pencil; a few miscellaneous anecdotes and a
superb passage about America. In justice to Anderson this last should be quoted. Perhaps never
before has one side of the American psychology
been so well summarized:

"In America . . . something went wrong in the
beginning. We pretended to so much and were
going to do such great things here. This vast
land was to be a refuge for all the outlawed brave
foolish folk of the world. The declaration of the
rights of man was to have a new hearing in a new
place. The devil! We did get ourselves into a
bad hole. We were going to be superhuman and
it turned out we were sons of men who were not
such devilish fellows after all. You cannot blame

us that we are somewhat reluctant about finding out the very human things concerning ourselves. One does so hate to come down off the perch.

"We are now losing our former feeling of inherent virtue, are permitting ourselves occasionally to laugh at ourselves for our pretensions, but there was a time here when we were sincerely in earnest about all this American business, 'the land of the free and the home of the brave.' We actually meant it and no one will ever understand present-day America or Americans who does not concede that we meant it and that while we were building all of our big ugly hurriedly-thrown-together towns, creating our great industrial system, growing always more huge and prosperous, we were as much in earnest about what we thought we were up to as were the French of the thirteenth century when they built the cathedral of Chartres to the Glory of God.

"They built the cathedral of Chartres to the glory of God and we really intended building here a land to the glory of Man, and thought we were doing it too. That was our intention and the affair only blew up in the process, or got perverted, because Man, even the brave and the free Man, is somewhat a less worthy object of glorification than God. This we might have found out long ago but that we did not know each other. We came from too many different places to know each other well, had been promised too much, wanted too much. We were afraid to know each other.

"Oh, how Americans have wanted heroes, wanted brave simple fine men! And how sincerely and deeply we Americans have been afraid to understand and love one another, fearing to find ourselves at the end no more brave, heroic and fine than the people of almost any other part of the world."

The short fourth book tells how it feels to become a successful writer, to go to New York and meet all the important literary people, and to take a trip to Europe. The book ends with an epilogue in which Anderson describes the visit to him of a successful writer of football stories who wants to go in for something a little more "artistic."

A Story Teller's Story is one of the most interesting documents that has come out of America in the last two decades. A hundred years from now it will still be a valuable source book. It will describe in abundant detail the psychological and emotional reactions of a super-sensitive, sentimental melodramatic man who was unable to adjust himself to an industrialized America. It will show a number of the processes whereby America changed from an incongruous, jumbled "melting pot" into a homogeneous nation with as definite a character and as varied idiosyncrasies as those of any European nation. And it will show the hardships worked upon unadaptable individuals by this process of standardization and assimilation. *A Story Teller's Story* may well be Anderson's most enduring book; it is perhaps the least pretentious of his works, but it comes closer to achieving its purpose than anything else he has written.

As Anderson explains in the preface, *Tar* started out to be an autobiographical account of his boyhood told in the first person, but that method of attack proved unsatisfactory, so he called himself "Tar" Moorehead and went on with the story. It is a remarkable testimonial to Anderson's craftsmanship that *Tar* is readable. In it he merely retells the same childhood that he has described so often before; the characters, the atmosphere, the feeling are identically the same. Yet the incidents are different and somehow one is not much oppressed by a sense of repetition.

Tar himself is an idealized memory. There never was, never could have been a boy like that. Anderson remembers the events of his boyhood, but he has forgotten the emotions he had. What the book achieves is a description of what the mature Anderson would have felt had he been able to reënact the events of his childhood. The agony, the sordidness, the ecstasy, the indescribable importance of unimportant events, the vividness of all emotional reactions are passed over. The young Tar possesses a saneness, a philosophical impassiveness that no child ever enjoyed, and certainly not such a child as was the hyper-sensitive Anderson. In short, the character of Tar has been so idealized that it is flat.

What one carries away from the book is the memory of a series of sharp, vivid snapshots: the death of the old woman in the snowstorm, the white body in the moonlight, the dogs running in a circle around her; Tar's shy love for the Farley girl and his idealization of her; his adventure with Mame Thompson in the hayloft, his fright and loss of nerve and later shame and regret that he lost his nerve; the loneliness of the "bad" woman, her affection for Tar and his understanding of her; the night the train came in late when Tar, accompanied by his restless sister, delivered his papers after midnight; their walk through the cemetery on the black rainy night, the sound of groaning, the flash of lightning that showed Hawkins, the filthy hog dealer, praying in the rain beside his wife's grave; Tar's glimpse through the back window of the drug clerk's house as the latter and his wife are making love; the contrast between the poverty of the Mooreheads with their thin cabbage stew and the abundance of food on the tables of Tar's friends; the evening when Tar's father came home drunk to an embarrassed, silent, frightened family. Tar himself is never quite real, but many of the things he does are.

Anderson's material is thinner, but he squeezes more out of what he has.

Sherwood Anderson's Notebook resembles suspiciously a collection of pot boilers. Most of the essays and sketches in it had been previously printed in such magazines as *The Nation, The New Republic, Vanity Fair, The Dial.* There is little in the volume that warrants detailed discussion. The essay entitled *A Note on Realism* is an interesting presentation of Anderson's literary philosophy, but we can consider that to better advantage a little further on. For the rest, the book contains rather insipid extracts, apparently from Anderson's diary; sketches of Gertrude Stein, Paul Rosenfeld, Ring Lardner, Sinclair Lewis, George Bellows and Alfred Stieglitz; and a few other miscellaneous essays.

POETRY

Two of Anderson's books, *Mid-American Chants* and *A New Testament*, may most easily be classified as poetry. They are unlike his usual prose; they are not essays; they very patently echo many of Walt Whitman's thoughts; they attempt to recapture the rhythm of certain passages from the Old Testament; and they bear evidence to a lyrical urge on the author's part.

Anderson himself presents them with modesty. In the foreword to *Mid-American Chants* he writes, "For this book of chants I ask only that it be allowed to stand stark against the background of my own place and generation. . . . In secret a million men and women are trying, as I have tried here, to express the hunger within and I have dared put these chants forth only because I hope and believe that they may find an answering and clearer call in the hearts of other Mid-Americans."

I am inclined to class these two volumes as clever and sometimes interesting experiments with new combinations of sounds and new methods of expression. Without defining the nebulous boundaries of poetry, I would say that these books carry prose perilously close to poetry. But they remain prose, they remain experimental, they remain confused, and despite their occasional cleverness they are never successful enough to make one forget that essentially they are *tours de force*. I think of Anderson writing them to blow off steam—because he has been feeling the limitations and restrictions of the usual prose forms, because he is exasperated at life or at something that has happened, because by employing this new medium he is able to consolidate and concentrate more than in prose, or merely because he feels poetic and thinks that he should be writing poetry.

The "poems" vary in mood and in quality quite as much as Anderson's other writing. Many of them voice the hysterical complaining wail of a baffled and defeated man, as, for instance, this passage from *Chicago:*

"I am a child, a confused child in a confused
    world. There are no clothes made that fit me.
    The minds of men cannot clothe me. Great
    projects arise within me. I have a brain and
    it is cunning and shrewd.
I want leisure to become beautiful, but there
    is no leisure. Men should bathe me with
    prayers and with weeping, but there are no
    men."

Most of these poems deal to some extent with the difficulty the artist has in combating the crass blatant ugliness of industrial life. In the *Song of Industrial America* Anderson catches that note especially well:

"They tell themselves so many little lies, my be-
      loved. Now wait, little one—we can't sing.
      We are standing in a crowd, by a bridge, in
      the West. Hear the voices—turn around—
      let's go home—I'm tired. They tell them-
      selves so many little lies.
You remember in the night we arose. We were
      young. There was smoke in the passage and
      you laughed. Was it good—that black
      smoke? Look away to the streams and the
      lake. We're alive. See my hand—how it
      trembles on the rail.
Here is song, here in America, here now, in our
      time. Now wait—I'll go to the train. I'll
      not swing off into tunes. I'm all right—I
      just want to talk. . . .
You know my city—Chicago triumphant—fac-
      tories and marts and the roar of machines—
      horrible, terrible, ugly and brutal.
It crushed things down and down. Nobody
      wanted to hurt. They didn't want to hurt
      me or you. They were caught themselves.
      I know the old men here—the millionaires.
      I've always known old men all my life. I'm
      old myself. You would never guess how old
      I am.

> Can a singer arise and sing in this smoke and
>   grime? Can he keep his throat clear? Can
>   his courage survive?
> I'll tell you what it is—now you be still. To Hell
>   with you. I'm an old empty barrel floating
>   in the stream—that's what I am. You stand
>   away. I've come to life. My arms lift up—
>   I begin to swim.
> Hell and damnation—turn me loose. The floods
>   come on. That isn't the roar of the trains at
>   all. It's the flood—the terrible, horrible
>   flood turned loose."

Several of the chants are hackneyed, sentimental and obviously derived, as, for instance,
Song to the Sap:

> "In my breasts the sap of spring,
> In my brain gray winter, bleak and hard,
> Through my whole being, surging strong and
>   sure,
> The call of gods,
> The forward push of mystery and of life . . .
>
> From all of Mid-America a prayer,
> To newer, braver gods, to dawns and days,
> To truth and cleaner, braver life we come.
> Lift up a song,
> My sweaty men,
> Lift up a song."

A New Testament is even more introspective,
sentimental and technically experimental than the

first volume of poems. Anderson is worrying about himself, attempting to analyze his reactions to people and to life in general, to decide what he is and what things are and what the relations between them actually are. In the process he comes to identify himself with trees, houses, streets, people, landscapes, thoughts, cities.

"At times, just for a moment, I am a Cæsar, a Napoleon, an Alexander. I tell you it is true.

"If you men who are my friends and those of you who are acquaintances could surrender yourselves to me for just a little while.

"I tell you what—I would take you within myself and carry you around with me as though I were a pregnant woman."

Most of Anderson's confessions and musings are confused and lushly sentimental. His baffledness over the meaning of life; his consciousness that he might have been a great writer and that he has not made full use of his potentialities; his flooding, overflowing sympathy for things in general and the difficulty he finds in fixing it on the concrete; his wistful romanticism; his insight into things and his inability to group his perceptions into a cohesive unity; his almost psychopathic introspection—all find their outlet here and combine to give us a picture of the baffled "pregnant" man who is Sherwood Anderson. But often before Anderson has given us this picture; it pours out of each book he has written. There is nothing new in what he says; it is merely said more sentimentally. One can understand how in a period of unusual bewilderment or depression he may have written these poems; school and college boys often have the same impulse; one wonders that he should publish them as they are.

There are, however, a few amusing experiments with word pictures, of which the following, from *Song Number Four*, is a good example:

"You are a small man sitting in a dark room in the early morning. Look, you have killed a woman. Her body lies on the floor. Her face is white and your hands tremble. A testament is creeping from between your teeth. It makes your teeth chatter.

You are a young man in the schools.

You walk up the face of a hill.

You are an insane driver of sheep.

You are a woman in a brown coat, a fish merchant in a village, a man who throws coal in at the mouth of a furnace, a maiden who presses the body of her lover against the face of the wall.

You are a bush.

You are a wind.

You are the gun of a soldier.

You are the hide that has been drawn over the face of a drum.

You are a young birch tree swaying in a wind.

You are one who has been slain by a falling tree in a forest.

Your body has been destroyed by a flying mass of iron in the midst of a battle.

Your voice comes up out of a great confusion.
Listen, little lost one, I am testifying to you as
I creep along the face of a wall. I am making a
testament as I gather stones and lay them along
the face of a wall."

There can be no doubt that these lines have a
certain effectiveness. It is as though a dozen
movie reels had been cut haphazardly, stuck together, and run flickering over the screen many
times too fast but occasionally coming to a full
stop. It is interesting to see that this effect can
be produced with words, but it is not especially
enlightening. Anderson has made public a lab-
oratory experiment that has not yet and is not
likely to come to a definite end.

III. IN RETROSPECT

ANDERSON has little reason to complain at the reception he has had at the hands of the American reading public. His books have been bought and read; the critics have treated him seriously and, for the most part, sympathetically; he is generally recognized to be one of the important contemporary writers; his books are recommended to foreigners who enquire about the present state of American literature, and they are beginning to be translated. His position and his reputation are such that it is no longer necessary to consider his works entirely tentatively.

It has been the habit of American critics in speaking of him to remark about succeeding volumes as they have appeared, "In this new work there are plain foreshadowings of the Anderson who is ahead." Anderson has published thirteen books. Perhaps it is not out of place to enquire just how much of a contribution to American literature these volumes seem to represent.

From this point of view, as we run again through the list of his works, we must strike off first of all his two volumes of poems. They show promise of a certain sort, but they most certainly fail to come up to a very high standard of accomplishment. With them, and for the same reason, must go *Tar* and four out of his five novels. In

The Triumph of the Egg and *Horses and Men*
perhaps half a dozen or eight short stories escape
the blue pencil. We have left: *Dark Laughter*,
A Story Teller's Story and *Winesburg, Ohio*.
The first is a competent novel, but it is no better
than many others that have appeared in America
in the last fifteen years; it is well written, but not
enough so to mark Anderson as an outstanding
writer. It is a little more difficult to place *A Story
Teller's Story*; one is never sure how much of its
interest is due to the publicity the author has
received and to a natural curiosity on the part of
the reader to know about him. We can class it
as an interesting book of reminiscences, but it is
doubtful whether it warrants a very high literary
rating. That leaves us with *Winesburg, Ohio*;
and *Winesburg*, limited and incomplete as it is,
seems, to my mind, a definite contribution to
American literature. As a first volume of short
stories it entirely justified the hopes, so often expressed, that at last there had developed in America a "home-bred," un-Anglicized writer who
would take his place beside the great writers. But
Anderson has not progressed; on the contrary,
each succeeding volume makes it seem less likely
that he will fulfill the great things that were expected of him. From time to time since the publication of *Winesburg* he has shown evidence of his
qualities of greatness, but seldom for more than
fleeting moments.

To paraphrase the author, "something is wrong
with Anderson's writing, and Anderson himself

doesn't want to look at it." After nine years of constant writing and the publication of ten subsequent books, his reputation still rests upon his first volume of short stories, and not thus supported, it would be negligible. We can find no more suitable point from which to undertake a discussion of his shortcomings than his essay, *A Note on Realism,* in which he voices his literary philosophy.

"There is something," he writes, "very confusing to both readers and writers about the notion of realism in fiction. As generally understood it is akin to what is called 'representation' in painting. The fact is before you and you put it down, adding a high spot here and there to be sure. . . . No man can quite make himself a camera. Even the most realistic worker pays some tribute to what is called 'art.' Where does representation end and art begin? . . .

"Easy enough to get a thrill out of people by reality. A man struck by an automobile, a child falling out at the window of an office building. Such things stir the emotions. No one, however, confuses them with art.

"This confusion of the life of the imagination with the life of reality is a trap into which most of our critics seem to fall about a dozen times each year. Do the trick over and over and in they tumble. 'It is life,' they say. 'Another great artist has been discovered.'

"What never seems to come quite clear is the simple fact that art is art. It is not life.

"The life of the imagination will always remain separated from the life of reality. It feeds upon the life of reality, but it is not that life—cannot be. Mr. John Marin painting Brooklyn Bridge, Henry Fielding writing *Tom Jones*, are not trying in the novel and the painting to give us reality. They are striving for a realization in art of something out of their own imaginative experiences, fed to be sure upon the life immediately about. A quite different matter from making an actual picture of what they see before them.

"And here arises a confusion. For some reason —I myself have never exactly understood very clearly—the imagination must constantly feed upon reality or starve. Separate yourself too much from life and you may at moments be a lyrical poet, but you are not an artist. Something within dries up, starves for want of food. Upon the fact in nature the imagination must constantly feed in order that the imaginative life remain significant. The workman who lets his imagination drift off into some experience altogether disconnected with reality, the attempt of the American to depict life in Europe, the New Englander writing of cowboy life—all that sort of thing—in ninety-nine cases out of a hundred ends in the work of such a man becoming at once full of holes and bad spots. The intelligent reader, tricked often enough by the technical skill displayed in hiding the holes, never in the end accepts it as good work. The imagination of the workman has become confused. He has had to depend altogether upon tricks. The whole job is a fake."

Anderson has stated the case with sufficient clearness. "Art is art. It is not life." Neither is it imagination of the type displayed by the New Englander describing cowboys—and neither is it imagination of the type displayed by Anderson when he sentimentally remakes the world according to his own measurements. Anderson writing about women, Anderson writing about most sexual phenomena, Anderson writing about philosophies of life, Anderson writing about Beauty, Truth, Love, Purity and other abstractions is in the same category with the New Englander writing about cowboys. They are both projecting qualities that they miss in life into something they know little about.

Anderson realizes the danger of writing from a notebook, but he fails to realize that similar faults may spring out of writing from an undisciplined imagination. At the risk of being boring, I would repeat that there are two kinds of imagination. One is powerful enough to penetrate completely, sympathetically into the world, or into some part of the world, as it exists. It we might call the interpretive imagination. The other is forced to create a world of its own as it is unable to understand and sympathize with the one that exists. In his conception of the stories in *Winesburg, Ohio*, and for brief moments in some of his other books, Anderson shows that he possesses this interpretive imagination. But most of his work is the product of that lower order of imagination that must remake the world in accordance with its own limitations.

In discussing realism and "art," Anderson fails to realize that it is of slight importance whether or not a writer makes an "actual picture" of what he sees. It may be that what one man sees is so grouped and arranged that by portraying it as it is the writer expresses that which he desires; it may be that to achieve such a result he will be forced to combine, rearrange and reconstruct. In this same essay Anderson gives a concrete example of the confusion under which he labors. He remarks that he sees a man walking down the street and wants to use him in a story. But to use this man as he is is too "realistic." "A matter easy enough to correct. A stroke of my pen saves me from realism. The man I knew in life had red hair; he was tall and thin. With a few words I have changed him completely. He has black hair and a black mustache. He is short and has broad shoulders. And now he no longer lives in the world of reality. He is a denizen of my own imaginative world." In short he isn't the red-haired man at all but "two other fellows." It is not that it matters whether the man is short or tall, red or black haired. Anderson by taking him into his own "imaginative world" has begun to distort him. In almost all of his writing he continues the process. When the man would really do one thing, Anderson makes him do another. Because he is not reproducing facts, he feels that he

is writing imaginatively. He is not. To lie about
life is not to write with imagination, but without
it.

Anderson has never needed to be "saved from
realism." He needs to be saved from a cheap,
soft sentimentality that distorts and castrates almost everything he writes. He has the comparatively rare gift of stating human problems validly; but once having stated them, he runs off,
hysterically frightened at what he has done. He
has sufficient insight into people, events, and emotions to broach a number of pertinent subjects,
but not once, even in *Winesburg*, has he carried
his investigations to the end without flinching.

It is hard and often grueling work to be a
creative writer, and Anderson has shirked the
task. He has done so because he has allowed himself to confuse the interpretive and the evasive
types of imagination that he possesses. How far
that confusion has gone is witnessed in the passage
just quoted in which he notes with surprise and
mystification that "art" is connected with and
derived from life. Had Anderson been writing as
he should and is able to write, he would be more
conscious of the fact that what he calls "art" is a
heightened and concentrated expression of the
emotional factors of life.

As we glance back through Anderson's works it
is striking to note what a large part of them is
devoted to sexual questions and relations. It is
even more striking to note that his only successful
treatment of this theme is when he depicts sexual

frustration. His other attempts to deal with it are ridiculously inadequate. Anderson would like to be a great historian of love but, to judge by his writings, his emotional experience is not great enough for the task. When he is not definitely dealing with sexual frustration, Anderson's attitude seems strangely akin to the one he attributes to Hugh McVey in *Poor White:* "It did not seem to him at the moment that it was worth while for him . . . to try to find a place . . . where such a wonderful thing as happened to the man in the barn (who kissed his fiancée) might happen to him."

And in a way complementary to this is Anderson's attitude toward women. Except for some of the studies in suppression in *Winesburg* he has never drawn a really convincing woman. He subconsciously places them on such a pedestal that he can't possibly treat them as human beings. Like David Ormsby in *Marching Men* we can hear him shout, "Women are not understandable. They do inexplicable things, have inexplicable fancies." One would say that he had indelibly stamped on his mind the traditional American and Victorian conception of marital virginity and purity which makes him write, as he does in *The Triumph of the Egg,* "The marriage night there was a brutal assault and after that the woman had to try to save herself as best she could." The nearest Anderson comes to acknowledging the fact that a woman can have normal emotions is when, in *Dark Laughter,* he writes stiltedly of Bruce Dudley that he could "be the man to her woman, for the moment at least."

Roughly, the subjects about which Anderson writes may be grouped as follows: He romantically rewrites his childhood and adolescence as it was or as it would have been pleasant had it been. He day-dreams on paper and tells himself fairy stories about "strong men" and "purposeful women" that make one wonder why the movies have never signed him up. He dramatizes, often sentimentally, stories or thoughts about the warped and deformed unfortunates whom modern life has left in its track. He tries to express the baffledness and mystification that he feels about ideals, sex, and the meaning of life—or else he tries to make some character solve these problems for him. He describes the physical background of contemporary America.

It is only when he is writing about frustration and in a few of his descriptions of the background of modern America that Anderson achieves any manner of success. The rest of the time one feels that he is writing for the pleasure of writing and not because he has anything to say. His dislike for modern life has dimmed his understanding of it and has left him in the unfortunate position of a reactionary who is trying to be and is often said to be a radical. His early experience left him bitter against commercialism, against the cheapness of quantity production, and convinced that no good can come of the present trend of life and that the only hope for the future is that the next generation may "reach down through all the broken surface distractions of modern life to that old love of craft out of which culture springs." (From *A Story Teller's Story*.) Anderson is a writer born out of his age.

It is doubtless noticeable that in this study little has been said of the other writers who seem to have influenced Anderson's work. This is largely because, although like almost all writers he has been influenced, he has absorbed and assimilated these influences until they have become indistinguishable from his ordinary views and reactions; and the process of searching out the sources of his methods and mannerisms throws little light on his writing itself. His early work owes a great deal to Dreiser's novels and to Whitman's feelings about America. The Old Testament has been very influential in the formation of his style, both in prose and poetry. There is a striking similarity between his theory of the history of life as a history of moments and the technique of Katherine Mansfield's short stories. The likeness of *Winesburg, Ohio* and some of his other writings to the work of the Russians, especially of Chekhov, has often been commented upon and, despite Anderson's repeated denials that he had read any Russian literature before the composition of *Winesburg*, it seems quite sure that, directly or indirectly, he was influenced by it. Be this as it may, the fact remains that Anderson is one of the most thoroughly and integrally American writers who has ever existed.

Sherwood Anderson, going into writing to escape from life, made one too-brief attempt to reenter life and then dashed frightened back to his refuge. In *Winesburg, Ohio,* and in parts of *The Triumph of the Egg* he seemed on the verge of penetrating imaginatively beneath the surface of this ugly, blatant life of ours and of tapping that rich vein of human nature which, changeless throughout the ages, has provided the stuff of all significant writing. But Anderson was unequal to the task. To the pure metal of genuine inspiration he preferred cheap substitutes, and so returned to his world of thin romanticism and sentimentality. The chance was his; we can but regret that he has not yet made real use of it.

BIBLIOGRAPHY

1916—Windy McPherson's Son.
1917—Marching Men.
1918—Mid-American Chants.
1919—Winesburg, Ohio.
1920—Poor White.
1921—The Triumph of the Egg.
1922—Many Marriages.
1923—Horses and Men.
1924—A Story Teller's Story.
1925—Dark Laughter.
1926—Sherwood Anderson's Notebook.
1926—"Tar," A Midwest Childhood.
1927—A New Testament.